Effective Innovation

Steven M. Bragg

AccountingTools®

ISBN 978-1-64221-182-5

For more information about AccountingTools® products, visit our Web site at www.accountingtools.com.

Table of Contents

About the Author

Steven Bragg, CPA, has been the chief financial officer or controller of four companies, as well as a consulting manager at Ernst & Young. He received a master's degree in finance from Bentley College, an MBA from Babson College, and a Bachelor's degree in Economics from the University of Maine. He has been a two-time president of the Colorado Mountain Club, and is an avid alpine skier, mountain biker, and certified master diver. Mr. Bragg resides in Centennial, Colorado. He has written more than 300 books and courses, including *New Controller Guidebook*, *GAAP Guidebook*, and *Payroll Management*.

Steven maintains the accountingtools.com web site, which contains continuing professional education courses, the Accounting Best Practices podcast, and thousands of articles on accounting subjects.

Effective Innovation

Introduction

If a business wants to generate above-average profits, then one of its most critical tools for doing so is being able to innovate. Doing so can yield fairly sustainable revenue and cost advantages, which can then be used to engage in further innovation to extend the positive effects. Given these advantages, why do so few senior managers give innovation their sustained backing? In many cases, they have done so in the past, but were frustrated with subpar results. In this book, we examine how to structure a system of innovation, where to concentrate the firm's efforts to achieve better results, and how to deal with a number of additional factors that can either enhance or torpedo the outcome.

Innovation Theory

The underlying concept behind the need to engage in innovation is to get better-performing and less-expensive goods and services into the hands of customers. This can be accomplished by a combination of changes in product design, the manufacturing process, and the value chain. This concept is derived from three assumptions, which are:

- *Unmet needs.* We assume that consumers have unmet needs that are waiting for a solution. Businesses need to constantly invest in innovation in order to discover these needs.
- *Value-based competition.* Businesses compete with each other based on the value of their offerings to consumers, where value is the ratio of product quality to price. Thus, innovation is needed to continually increase the level of value being offered. The usual outcome is either a commitment to offer the lowest price (with innovations targeted at cost reductions), or develop a high level of product quality (with innovations targeted at product features).
- *Business partner engagement.* In order to discover unmet needs and deliver value to consumers, a business needs to develop relationships with its business partners to conduct research, develop products, source parts, produce goods, distribute them, and provide after-market servicing. This requires varying degrees of trust-building between the parties, which will change over time as the organization's product mix evolves.

A potential problem with this classic view of innovation is that companies tend to pursue the best opportunities first, so that later innovation efforts are targeted at issues that are more likely to yield diminishing returns. This means that, *if* everyone is equally competent at the innovation process, then their pursuit of declining returns should result in approximate parity over the long term. There are multiple ways out of this trap, which are:

- *Pursue new markets*. Companies can pursue entirely new markets where there is no competition, allowing them to generate significant returns for long periods of time.
- *Refine innovation*. Not all companies are equally good at innovation. Some do not engage in it at all, while others have flawed processes. Consequently, a highly-refined and actively-supported process can deliver a long-term advantage to a business.
- *Embed with customers*. The company can provide a service so perfectly targeted at customers that they see no reason to switch their allegiance elsewhere, no matter how innovative the competition may be. This approach requires a business to develop deep relationships with its customers; this will likely result in a high level of information sharing with them, giving the company in-depth insights into what they need.
- *Create new value*. In most industries, innovation tends to cluster around specific areas, such as process improvements in the oil and gas industry. This tends to result in everyone coming up with the same innovations, which results in no competitive advantage. Instead, the company can come up with new areas in which to compete, such as when Cirque du Soleil altered the traditional circus away from animal acts and toward acrobatic feats. These fundamental shifts in how to perceive a market can result in significantly enhanced odds of generating unusually high returns.

The preceding trap avoidance recommendations are especially important when you consider that, in many established markets, the amount of revenue to be gained from each incremental innovation improvement tends to decline, because product cycles are shortening, leaving companies with less time in which to recoup their costs before the next iteration of products hits the market. Hence, the need to improve the innovation process.

Innovation Strategy

An organization's strategy can be thought of as a commitment to achieving a specific goal. The best strategies are designed to align the activities of each functional area of a business toward reaching the targeted goal. While there might be a great deal of attention paid to integrating the efforts of the traditional business areas in order to push a strategy forward, this is rarely the case with innovation. Instead, innovation tends to produce an assortment of unrelated best practices that have a modest impact on operations throughout the business. These improvements rarely have a direct impact on the corporate strategy, since there was never any intent for them to do so.

A better approach is to devise a more structured approach to innovation, where there is a coherent set of processes in place that mandate the areas in which the company is especially interested in looking for innovations, and the funding processes used to ensure that the best alternatives are provided with sufficient resources. Having such a system in place is especially important when there is limited funding available, since management needs to pick which innovation opportunities to provide with funding, where those decisions are based on how each one relates to the corporate strategy.

It can be useful to identify the areas in which business innovation can occur, in order to direct management's thinking into those areas where innovation will be most beneficial to the business. This approach is also useful for identifying neglected areas that could benefit from an enhanced level of innovation. The following areas can be used to segment the various opportunities:

- *Branding.* Where the company creatively leverages its brand, as Richard Branson has done by applying the Virgin brand to a vast array of businesses.
- *Custom solutions.* Where the company structures itself to offer tailored solutions to each of its customers. Any consulting firm uses this approach.
- *Customer experience.* Where the company completely overhauls the customer experience to make it as unobtrusive or delightful as possible. The high-end Mandarin Oriental hotel chain is firmly centered on this approach.
- *Development platform.* Where the company bases its product offerings on a central platform, from which it creates derivative products. Car companies operate in this area, where they build multiple car models on top of a single engine and drivetrain configuration.
- *Distribution channels.* Where the company finds unique channels to sell its products, such as high-end watches sold at ports of call for cruise ships, or kiosks in airport concourses.
- *Process efficiency.* Where the company increases its internal efficiencies in order to reduce costs. For example, Toyota's just-in-time production system greatly reduces its costs.
- *Product innovation.* Where the company devises unique new products and services, such as the iPhone.
- *Revenue sharing.* Where the company takes a share of the earnings from customer interactions. Mastercard and Visa use this approach by charging a fee whenever anyone uses one of their credit cards.
- *Supply chain.* Where the company creates a streamlined information flow back through its supply chain, so that parts and goods can be delivered as seamlessly as possible. For example, Dell Computer has long had a highly-refined system for acquiring parts on short notice from its supply base.
- *Underserved niches.* Where the company seeks out underserved market niches and fills them, usually with a high level of service and/or customization in order to ward off competitors.

When a business applies innovation to several of the preceding areas at once, then the profit effect tends to be multiplied. For example, Tesla has leveraged its battery technology into an array of products, while applying its brand to additional products, such as the Powerpack and solar roof tiles. Further, its distribution channel is direct to the customer, which goes around the traditional approach of selling through distributors.

Having an innovation strategy in place can be immensely useful when management is confronted on an almost a daily basis with requests from all over the company to engage in such activities as the acquisition of a new order entry system, the rollout of a new distribution channel, the acquisition of a promising start-up company, the development of a new product to fill out an existing product line, and so forth. By applying the strategy to these requests, management can focus on which ones will be of the most use in advancing the overall company strategy.

EXAMPLE

A company has significant expertise in developing land databases for different purposes, such as oil and gas leases and mining rights. The company routinely sells its products to large corporations at relatively high price points. A department manager presents management with a proposal to develop a GPS device that assists golfers in determining their exact distance from the hole. With a strong strategic vision, this proposal should be shot down, since it addresses a market far away from the company's core market, involves a hardware device instead of the company's usual database product, and will likely need to be sold at a relatively low price. [Author's note: this was a real situation; the company's CEO dabbled with the idea for several months before dropping it]

> **Note:** This more focused view of innovation strategy does not mean that a business cannot spread the innovation concept throughout the business, to harness the efforts of all employees – but the main thrust of the concept should be relatively focused in order to generate the greatest gains.

Ideally, an innovation strategy should allow management to focus on the following key areas when investigating innovation investments:

- *Value creation for customers*. An innovation should deliver some type of value for the company's customers, either by saving them more or providing them with new features for which they are willing to pay money. The targeted outcome might address such areas of interest to customers as durability, convenience, or cost reduction.
- *Profit creation for the company*. An innovation should allow the company to continue earning a profit. This might involve the development of a product ecosystem (combined with service and support) that customers will not be inclined to depart from. Or, innovation might be targeted at developing a sustainable cost advantage, to fend off products from lower-cost countries.
- *Types of applicable innovations*. The corporate strategy might mandate that innovation activities be targeted at a very specific part of the business, so that the results directly support the direction in which the company wants to go. For example, a distributor's strategic direction might mandate that innovations be focused on the development of a seamless ordering system for

customers, while an open-pit mining company might be more interested in innovations surrounding the automation of ore transport from the floor of the mine to the surface.

- *Broad perspective.* The corporate strategy could incorporate a broad perspective on the areas in which innovation can enhance the business. Thus, one should remain open to the possibility of addressing areas of innovation that competitors are ignoring, such as enhancing the customer experience in a coffee shop, or enhancing customer service in a car dealership.
- *Redefinition of the business case.* The corporate strategy could be redesigned to change the rules of the competitive game. This can be done by defining who customers are, *what* products should be offered to them, and *how* products should be offered to them.
- *Identification of uncertainties.* The corporate strategy should involve the identification of technical and market uncertainties, and address how to learn more about them. This approach is useful for prioritizing which uncertainties are the most important, developing a list of alternative outcomes for those uncertainties, and then testing them in order to resolve the uncertainties.

Innovation strategies will likely change over time. This is because any strategy is really just a hypothesis regarding the behavior of a targeted market, which might not prove to be valid. If customers, competitors, regulators, or technologies behave in unexpected ways, then a strategy will need to evolve to adapt to these realities.

Another viewpoint on innovation strategy is that it also involves the inverse – getting *rid of* business activities in order to free up the cash needed to invest in new innovations. This typically involves an examination of emerging trends to deduce changes in customer tastes, demography, regulatory, and political issues. Examples of such trends are switching away from blue jeans and toward yoga pants, or switching away from sedans and toward SUVs, or switching away from plane travel and toward anything more environmentally friendly. In particular, management needs to investigate the following issues on an iterative basis:

- On what conditions does our current success depend?
- Which of these conditions might change in the future?
- How can we prepare for these changes?

An examination of these issues can reveal insights into whether a company should exit certain business lines and focus its attention elsewhere.

EXAMPLE

A company that builds high-powered racing boats notices an increasing trend among customer inquiries, to see if the firm builds more environmentally-friendly electric boats. Management decides to exit its primary line of business over the next few years, and focuses all of its attention on building electric racing boats instead.

In this case, management spotted early indications that buying behavior was turning in a new direction, and decided to change the company's product offerings to match that behavior.

The grand strategy associated with exiting lines of business can fall into multiple areas, which are:

- *Specific timeframe.* Continue selling the current set of products and services for a specific period of time, and then switch over to new ones as of a predetermined date. This option is most likely when there are only a few possible alternative paths to take, and management is confident that it can predict the future with a relatively high degree of probability.
- *Early mover.* Continually examine the market for incipient changes in customer preferences, and be ready to innovate at once, moving away from the existing lines of business on short notice. This approach requires a significant investment in a range of innovations, in order to take advantage of being an early market entrant. This also means having high margins, since the firm may need to recoup its investments quickly if product lifespans prove to be short.
- *Researcher.* Have people in the marketplace, constantly looking for ideas that have been developed elsewhere, but which can be acquired or licensed for immediate use by the company. This approach works well if the company has developed a strong capability to bring ideas to market within a short period of time, and has the cash to acquire ideas from third parties. It is also helpful if the company can jump on new ideas quickly, before others recognize their value and drive up their price. In this case, a company may be more inclined to stay in its existing lines of business for as long as they generate enough cash flow, in order to fund outside acquisitions. When cash flows decline, these businesses are shut down.

Which of the preceding options to select is based on a variety of factors, including the financial position of the business, the staff time that is available for dealing with multiple initiatives, and how much the corporate culture is associated with existing products and services.

An innovation strategy must be properly funded. This means that the capital budgeting process is configured to grant funds on short notice to strategically-valuable projects, and that the funding allocated to innovation is always sufficient to pay for all projects that support the innovation strategy. Further, funding needs to be targeted at actual strategic innovations, rather than the favored projects of the various departments. This may call for mandated funding in targeted areas, such as 40% of all innovation funding for radical innovation projects.

EXAMPLE

The senior managers of a consumer electronics company see a long-term need for an innovation leap to a new technology platform, and communicate this need to the management team. After a year, little progress has been made. At that point, investigation into innovation funding reveals that the production manager demanded robotic production line investments to cut his costs, which in turn were driven by pressure from the accounting department, which wanted to preserve margins. In short, the long-term needs of the business were being sacrificed to meet short-term requirements.

A final point favoring the use of an innovation strategy is that it streamlines the process for deciding which proposed projects should be pursued and which should be dropped or deferred. When everyone knows the criteria for project selection, there tend to be far fewer arguments about whether a funding proposal should proceed.

> **Note:** Be sure to convince the board of directors of the need for ongoing innovation funding. Otherwise, they may retain the traditional focus on short-term results, and shortchange innovation in favor of other activities. Doing so requires that innovation be regularly listed on the board's agenda, and that board members have backgrounds in innovation activities or technology. It can also be useful for them to meet with key customers and/or attend industry conferences.

Strategic Innovation

It appears that we have merely swapped the words in the section header from the title in the preceding section. However, this topic is entirely different; in this case, we are looking at the use of strategic experiments within a business. A *strategic experiment* is a risky new venture being run within an established business. It is usually intended to be a multi-year investment in a market that is not well defined, and for which there is no obvious way to earn a profit. This situation arises most commonly in an emerging industry, where no one has a good idea of what the final outcome of the market will be. In this situation, the company that learns from its strategic experiments the most quickly will be the one most likely to capture the market.

When engaged in strategic innovation, a business will likely find that its initial expectations concerning a new market are incorrect – sometimes by orders of magnitude. To add to the ambiguity, it can be extraordinarily difficult to design strategic experiments that yield clear outcomes, because key variables cannot be perfectly isolated. For example, will increasing the price of a product by 50% really yield a clear outcome that sales therefore declined by 20%, or was the change in sales also impacted by seasonal sales differences or because the company changed its store location? Further, the outcome of experiments may take several years to become fully visible, and even then, the results may be ambiguous. Given these issues, managers should focus on the following factors to glean the maximum amount of information from a strategic experiment:

- *Focus on critical unknowns.* These are typically the cost structure needed to succeed in the market, the impact of technology, and the size and segmentation of the market.
- *Focus on the underlying assumptions.* Assumptions are used to build financial models for a new market. Rather than focusing on whether the initial set of revenue and expense assumptions turned out to be true, look instead at the assumptions used to derive these models. Refining the assumptions will lead to better modeling. For example, when entering a new market, it is impossible to know the number of customer support staff needed for every $10 million of sales; this is something that can be learned through a strategic experiment.
- *Focus on trends.* Examine the rate and direction of change, such as 10% increases in sales from quarter to quarter, rather than trying to predict exact revenue or expense amounts. Trends are relatively easy to derive, whereas predicting exact revenue or expense figures in a new market is nearly impossible. A markedly different trend than the amount expected could be grounds for a change in strategy.
- *Focus on leading indicators.* Identify any leading indicators linked to the market, since they provide early warning signs about whether the company's assumptions are realistic. For example, a leading indicator in the market for asteroid mining is likely to be the market price of the commodities to be mined – if these prices fall too low, then the cost-effectiveness of asteroid mining will be called into question.
- *Focus on updates.* Review the outcomes of strategic experiments quite frequently, such as on a monthly basis. The markets being investigated are likely changing rapidly, so management needs fresh information to evaluate performance and decide whether a strategic shift is needed. This approach can also keep a business from investing too much in a market that turns out to be smaller than expected.

The outcome of a strategic experiment is a strategic innovation, which represents a significant departure from historical practice in one of the following areas:

- *Design of the value chain.* A classic example is Dell Computer's sale of computers to customers, *after which* it built them. This resulted in negative working capital requirements, since it was paying its suppliers well after it received cash from its customers.
- *Conceptualization of delivered value.* For example, rather than selling completed jet engines to airlines, engine manufacturers sell hours of operating time to the airlines, and provide all ancillary services as part of this arrangement, such as engine monitoring and maintenance.
- *Identification of customers.* For example, Grameen Bank pioneered the extension of microlending to the poor in India, which was a market that had previously been completely ignored.

Innovation Predictions

When developing a plan for which areas to focus on for innovation enhancements, one would certainly be justified in spending some time in trying to predict the area in which the next breakthrough will occur. Making the correct call could put the company well ahead in the development of properly-positioned innovations, while a bad call could result in innovations that no one cares about. In order to improve your predictive abilities in this area, identify the evolutionary path of the technology under review. Consider the need that was originally being fulfilled by the technology, and then consider how each successive step along its evolutionary path brought it closer to answering the initial need. For example, one of the initial needs for a cell phone was portability, which was addressed to varying degrees over the years, as brick-sized devices were replaced by ever-lighter units. It would be reasonable to say at this point that there is little room left for portability to be improved upon. Similarly, the environmental impact of an automobile has resulted in the production of electric cars, for which a key consideration is miles per charge. At some point, perhaps at 1,000 miles per charge, this will no longer be a competitive factor for cars. Thus, when a 1,000-mile charge has been reached, the utility to the customer has been maximized, and additional mileage improvements beyond that point will probably not be significant to the customer.

From an innovation planning perspective, the clear path is to identify the key evolutionary paths associated with a product, and determine whether customer utility has been maximized. If so, eliminate them from consideration and focus your innovation efforts on those other areas in which improvement is still possible. This concept can be refined further by focusing on innovation at the intersection of where customers want to see more improvement and where the company's capabilities are the greatest.

In short, it is essential to keep tabs on the level of utility of the various dimensions of a product that are being provided to customers, and plan to shift toward new areas of improvement when the utility level being provided is close to the maximum that customers expect.

Closed Innovation

The traditional approach to organizing a system of innovation was to adopt the stance that all innovation must come from within. This meant that a business would hire the best and brightest into its own research lab, from which amazing product and process improvements would periodically emerge. Each of these improvements would then be commercialized, thereby funding yet more research and development spending – and so on. The company would then have complete control over the product, so that it could produce, market, and sell it using its own employees. Further, it would legally protect its intellectual property with patents, so that no competitors could benefit from it. In short, only the initial funding would be needed to pay for a research and development function, after which it would pay for itself.

While this approach can still be used, it suffers from a few problems. First, there is a strong market for researchers, so a competitor can hire them away, along with detailed knowledge of the company's intellectual property. Second, this process does not necessarily result in a predictable stream of profitable innovations. Instead, there may be long – quite long – intervals between the introduction of commercially viable products, so the research and development group might require substantially more funding than had initially been expected. And finally, just because a business has a long history of excellent product development does not mean that an upstart competitor cannot appear and quickly take away a large chunk of its business. Consequently, the closed innovation concept does not always work as well as might be expected. This brings us to the next topic, which is open innovation.

Open Innovation

When management decides to engage in an enhanced level of innovation, there is a tendency to invest significant resources internally, so that any solutions developed are entirely home-grown. This may seem like a major competitive advantage, since the innovations developed are not available anywhere else. Further, these innovations can represent a significant amount of intellectual property. Despite these obvious advantages to internal development, it can make even more sense to look outside the company for innovation ideas. Doing so provides the firm with access to a vast pool of knowledge that could not be replicated with any amount of internal investment, and so is more likely to result in a significant leap in performance that would not have otherwise occurred. Also, it can be much less expensive to tap into the research work already completed by other parties, rather than attempting to replicate it in-house.

There are several ways to engage in a more open innovation regime, including the following:

- *Benchmarking activities*. A business should institute an ongoing process of searching for better practices outside of the firm. This may involve perusing research papers, traveling to best practice businesses to see their operations, attending conferences, and so forth. A larger company might consider investing in its own network of scouts, to actively search for new ideas.
- *Cross-subsidiary sharing*. In a larger organization, one subsidiary may develop an improvement that should be shared across the organization. Doing so still keeps the knowledge relatively proprietary, while maximizing its usage within the organization. This is an especially useful approach when the subsidiaries make similar products, so innovations are more likely to be applicable across the organization. Cross-subsidiary sharing can be accomplished with a formal knowledge sharing program, including periodic meetings, plant tours, and a best practices database to exchange information.
- *Implementation speed*. When using innovations found outside the company, this implies that the company will only be catching up to what is already being done elsewhere. However, by increasing the speed of innovation implementation over that of competitors, the firm can still experience a

competitive advantage, even when everyone is merely accessing the same best practices.

- *Leading off-the-shelf software*. Many of the more sophisticated off-the-shelf software packages already include best practices that the software providers have learned from their interactions with hundreds of customers. These packages are available for all parts of a business, including systems for warehouse management, customer relationships, and (at a more expansive level) enterprise resource planning systems. By fully installing these software packages and considering all options available, management can significantly improve company operations.
- *On-site tours*. It can be quite helpful to conduct in-depth customer tours of the company's facilities, so that employees can learn from customers regarding exactly what they want. This can lead to additional changes in the methods of production and product designs that are more in line with customer expectations.
- *Licensing*. When the company develops something that is outside of its normal area of production, marketing or distribution expertise, it can license the rights to a third party. Doing so ensures that some revenue will still be gained, even if the firm does not exploit the knowledge internally. This approach can be expanded through the enforcement of a company policy that requires all ideas to be licensed out if they are not used internally within a certain number of years. Doing so frees up the value associated with the ideas. Conversely, the company may elect to license outside knowledge for use internally, in which case it will need to pay licensing fees to someone else.

In regard to the last point about licensing innovations to other parties, this is a logical outgrowth of the market positioning, resources, and management interests of a company. There may be significant differences in how companies even in the same industry view these factors, so that certain innovations may be more applicable to one business than another. Consequently, a business might develop an interesting concept, but does not believe that it fits the pattern that has proven to be successful for it in the past; rather than struggling with rolling out the idea, they hand it off to another party (for a fee), so that the business still profits from it to some extent.

Innovation Partnerships

A business may find that it can carve out a unique innovation niche by working with its customers to develop customized, cost-effective solutions for them. Doing so has three advantages. First, the company is assured of generating sales from its efforts, since the resulting products and services will be sold directly into the partnering entities. Second, the company is in a good position to lock in these customers in the future, as long as it continues to work with them on future innovations. The result is ongoing increases in sales that are driven by a relatively locked-in customer base. And finally, the company gains insights into customer-specific issues that may not have been addressed by competitors who have not spent as much time delving into customer needs; this can yield a technological edge. This edge can be increased by deliberately seeking out those customers with the most challenging needs, and learning from their requirements.

The preceding benefits can be expanded upon if the company decides to build upon what it has learned through its customer partnerships, to develop products that are more broadly applicable to a larger market. This involves poring over localized innovation projects to extract those elements that the company expects will be desirable features for other firms in the same market. This approach can greatly increase total sales, but it may not be quite as successful, since the company is not developing innovation partnerships with this new group of customers. Instead, it will be seen as just another competitor, though perhaps with a somewhat better set of product features than those of its rivals.

Yet another type of innovation partnership arises when a business works with the nonprofit and government sectors to customize its products to meet their priorities. This arrangement may not result in outsized profits, but it can build substantial amounts of goodwill, which can result in preferential treatment, or at least the company's inclusion in protected areas of laws applying to a specific market. For example, a car company could elect to build a research center within a city that is suffering from a high level of unemployment, and which will require that a number of high-paying positions be filled. As another example, a business could work with a leading university to jointly operate an innovation lab. This approach is especially useful if management anticipates that the company might come under public scrutiny at some point in the future; such proactive efforts tend to mitigate political risks.

In effect, the stages described here involve starting at the periphery of a market and gradually moving towards its center, building expertise where other competitors are not doing so, and then protecting the increased market share with ongoing joint initiatives.

Innovation in a Fluid Environment

A company may be faced with a situation in which its industry is in an unsettled state, such as when new competitors are entering the industry with unique products, or when the traditional market appears to be failing. In these cases, it can make sense to move innovation outside of the company and engage in partnering with other businesses. The firm may act as an orchestrator, bringing together multiple partners to discuss entirely new products or processes. These partners may be from outside the industry, but have competencies that could make sense when integrated into a new product or service. Thus, a drone manufacturer could be brought in to an operation in Africa that is tasked with delivering blood and medical supplies to villages that cannot be easily reached in a timely manner. The use of drones for these deliveries represents a completely new application for the drone manufacturer, while the local delivery service is unable to deliver the needed goods without access to the drones. In this case, both partners can profit from their joint activities.

This approach works well when a problem and its solution need to be clarified. To return to the preceding example, the blood delivery company reaches out to the drone manufacturer to explore such matters as the weight that can be carried, the distances that can be flown, whether drones can fly autonomously, and the operating cost of the drones. The answers gleaned from this discussion can then be used to decide whether an opportunity exists.

When developing a network of partners for this type of innovation, the orchestrator needs a system for finding possible partners and then winnowing them down to a manageable group. This can be accomplished by organizing networking events to which potential partners and experts are invited to discuss problem areas. These discussions can be used to gauge whether prospective partners are valuable to the orchestrator. When a new partner proves to indeed be valuable in partnering arrangements, it is then more likely that the orchestrator will use that partner again, resulting in a core group of innovation partners that work together on multiple projects.

The partners in an innovation group rarely use tightly-structured contracts that specify such matters as due dates and price points. Instead, they operate under agreements that merely set forth the general boundaries of contemplated operations, and the expected contributions of each party. As more precise business models eventually take shape, these agreements are then refined to address the more specific operating characteristics of the obligations and deliverables of the various parties.

The end result of innovations in a fluid environment is likely to be an expanded use of partnerships, rather than the in-house innovation structures commonly found in businesses competing within established markets. This partnership approach can work well even in environments that are less fluid, since exposure to other businesses expands management's view of what is possible, both internally and within their markets. Also, having the capability to work with partners is a skill that can be used to develop a shifting set of partners to deal with the various uncertainties that a business will encounter over its life.

Innovation and Company Size

Larger enterprises have great difficulty in creating a stream of innovations. There are several reasons for this, which are:

- *Status quo*. A larger company has a commensurately large market share, and so has an interest in maintaining the status quo. This is because it is designed to maximize profits as the industry is currently structured, so any change to that structure will reduce its profits. It is organizationally structured to produce the existing set of products and services via current distribution channels. Innovations tend to disrupt this structure, and so can meet with vigorous resistance.
- *Bureaucracy*. A large business has likely built up several additional layers of management, as well as administrative staff in such areas as capital budgeting, safety, human resources, and risk management. While each decision to incrementally add these people to the company might make sense, the overall effect is similar to pouring sand into a motor – everything slows down. When

there is a strong bureaucratic effect, it can be quite difficult to devise innovations on a consistent basis.

- *Large-scale orientation.* Larger companies can set aside significant amounts of funds for innovations, usually with the intent of pursuing blockbuster new products. These types of projects tend to receive the bulk of all funding. However, these strategies frequently do not pay off, since they are, by definition, high risk. In short, businesses that bet big also tend to lose big. In addition, with most of their R&D funding allocated to these blockbuster projects, there is comparatively little funding left for smaller, lower-risk innovation projects.

A common way for a large business to avoid these problems is to enter into research partnerships with smaller companies and start-up businesses, and then buy up these partners or just license their products when a useful innovation has been produced. By using this approach, a larger firm essentially outsources its research, while focusing on what it does best, which is more likely to be in such areas as production, distribution, and/or marketing. Ideally, a large company might be associated with a dozen or more small companies in research partnerships.

A variation on the outsourced research concept is to fund a separate organization that is entirely focused on providing innovation to the business. This research group is typically housed separately from the rest of the company, because management does not want the rest of the organization's inertia to have a negative impact on it. Also, the manager to whom this organization reports may be the chief executive officer or some other very senior member of management; with such high-level support, it is difficult for lower-level managers to negatively influence ongoing innovation activities.

Characteristics of Successful Innovators

Some people are much better at delivering high-quality innovations that can be readily implemented than others. What sets apart these successful innovators? Here are several characteristics that they typically share:

1. *Network the problem.* A successful innovator usually farms out the problem, rather than trying to solve it initially by himself. This means discussing the issue with associates to gain a better understanding of the underlying problem, especially when someone else has a different perspective on the issue.
2. *Establish mutual benefit.* A successful innovator does a good job of showing the other members of his network what the mutual benefit would be to all parties of finding a good solution to the problem. Doing so creates more of an incentive for others to search for a high-quality solution, since they will benefit from it.
3. *Obtain feedback.* A successful innovator realizes that the first idea generated is probably not perfect, and so will solicit feedback from others. The intent is to poke holes in ideas as soon as possible, in order to spend minimal time focusing on the wrong solutions. Consequently, it is necessary to pull in

naysayers very early in a process and consult with them regularly as additional ideas are generated. Eventually, after multiple rounds of debate, the entire group will have bought into the final solution, thereby creating a group of backers who will support it.

4. *Market the idea.* A successful innovator understands that a large part of the process of innovation development is selling the idea to the organization. This means spending a substantial amount of time developing a narrative with which people will connect. At this stage, the innovator can expect to make a number of additional tweaks to the idea being presented, as the concept is rolled out to a larger audience that brings up additional concerns.

A key point in this discussion is that the best innovators are bringing in other parties to participate in innovation projects as soon as the initial problem surfaces, and continue to do so throughout the innovation process. A high degree of buy-in is essential to the eventual success of an innovation, so the involvement of many parties in a project is critical.

Unconventional Thinking

Frequently, the best innovations come from unconventional thinking, where a person steps far outside of the normal strictures associated with a problem, to view the situation from an entirely different perspective. What activities does an unconventional thinker engage in to develop a groundbreaking innovation? Here are some of the more common requirements:

- They like to step back from the tactical considerations of a problem to gain perspective on the bigger picture. This may involve challenging their current notions regarding solutions to problems, which is easier for someone who is not already an expert in the field. This could require a significant period of time, while they reflect upon the nature of the underlying problem. They need to spend time away from their regular jobs in order to enter into the amount of contemplation needed for breakthrough solutions.

- They spend time tinkering with unorthodox solutions or combinations of solutions, which inherently requires them to question accepted practices and assumptions. In product development, this may involve the exploration of uses of the company's products in unique ways, to see if solutions have already been devised by customers.

- They conduct experiments quickly and at low cost, so that they can address a larger number of potential options. They are accustomed to failure on numerous experiments, from which they learn more about the problem. These experiments may be conducted with customers, who can provide valuable feedback regarding failure points that need to be corrected.

- They spend considerable effort on introducing and delivering their solutions. They realize that their solutions may be so "out there" that user acceptance will be difficult, so they anticipate user arguments and devise the appropriate framing to increase the odds of success. This also means that they do not disclose information about their work until they are ready to support it with appropriate arguments, thereby keeping critics from getting started early on shooting it down.

This will likely involve a nonlinear path from the initial idea to a possible solution, quite possibly requiring multiple iterations as different ideas are explored and cast aside. At each iteration, the individual is gaining knowledge – even if it is only about what will *not* work – which can then be used to improve upon the next idea. It is difficult to discern a specific process flow when unconventional thinking is used to create innovative new ideas, so do not try to develop a specific procedure for it, with rigid start points and milestone reviews at certain intervals. Instead, it is a more fluid process that will change over time.

Asking the Right Questions

Rather than trying to dream up nifty new solutions that are not needed by customers, it can be more useful to spend some time devising the questions that need to be solved. This approach avoids one of the main problems with brainstorming, which is making suggestions that will be shot down by other attendees; posing questions tends to be less confrontational. Here are several tips for doing so:

1. *Invite outsiders.* Invite people to participate who have no experience with the issue at hand. They have a different worldview, and so are more likely to come up with unique questions, because they are not invested in the status quo.
2. *Lay out the problem.* Briefly describe the nature of the problem to the attendees, and why it has not yet been resolved.
3. *Collect questions.* Only allow questions relating to the problem, not solutions. The search is for surprising and potentially provocative questions, as well as to collect a large number of questions within just a few minutes.
4. *Review and select questions.* Examine the questions to see if any of them hint at avenues worth exploring that could resolve the underlying problem. For this reduced set of questions, ask yourself why they seem important, in order to better understand why it really matters.
5. *Take action.* Commit to follow up on one of the action paths suggested by one of the questions, and develop an action plan for doing it.

EXAMPLE

A project manager has been having difficulty rolling out a quality control best practice at the company's 40+ manufacturing locations. During a question brainstorming session, someone asks why she could not issue a training video to the local managers and have them do the installation? This leads to several follow-on questions, including why the project manager has not considered this approach before, and whether she has a problem with delegating responsibility.

As an action plan, she schedules several sessions with a therapist to explore whether she has an excessively controlling nature that is interfering with her delegation of work.

In the preceding example, the action outcome was entirely different from what the manager probably expected when she initiated the problem brainstorming session.

Incremental Innovation

Incremental innovation occurs when management elects to make small, iterative improvements. This approach has a high success rate, since innovations are built upon business models that already work, and which have an existing pool of customers. Also, these "tweaking" changes tend to be relatively inexpensive, so a business can generate reasonable returns from incremental innovations, with a relatively low risk of failure. A further advantage to engaging in incremental innovation is that these changes pile up – a series of small upgrades to a product over a period of time could result in a product that is considered a game changer when compared to the competition.

There is an investment philosophy associated with incremental innovation. Since each incremental innovation effort is not that expensive, a business can develop a broad-ranging portfolio of small individual bets on innovation. A few will not generate a return, but most should do quite well. This is a better alternative than investing a large amount in a small number of innovation initiatives, since just a few failures here will result in a drastically reduced return on investment.

A good way to create a more effective incremental innovation campaign is to apply the principles of target costing to research and development activities, where a project team investigates the cost required to improve a product, and how much more customers will be willing to pay for the resulting incremental improvement. The result is a replacement product that generates more value for the company. A variation is to create value through cost reduction, where an innovation results in a less-expensive product that will generate a higher profit margin for the company.

A highly targeted approach is to build incremental innovation on top of a more disruptive innovation. For example, Amazon's release of the Kindle e-book reader (definitely disruptive) was followed by a number of improvements, including a touch screen and several sizes of readers (all incremental improvements). The initial version of a disruptive technology tends to be a bit rough, which presents the opportunity for a series of incremental improvements.

Businesses tend to confuse the concept of incremental innovation with issuing a massive number of slightly different product variations, in hopes of conquering every possible product niche. While this approach may increase sales in the short term, it also creates a substantial logistical challenge, since the company must now maintain a much larger number of stock-keeping units, which may adversely impact its profits. A better approach is to maintain roughly the same number of products, but to retire older and less profitable versions when more profitable replacements are rolled out.

Innovation Enablers

When working on possible solutions to a problem, a common issue is that a person tends to fixate on the current proposed solution, which does little for the generation of a range of alternatives. An excellent way to mitigate this fixation problem is to schedule a number of breaks or other distractions during the day. A break is especially useful, because it reduces the recency value of inappropriate ideas. Logically, a longer break is better than a shorter one, since it has a more profound impact on the recency of ideas. A variation is to shift to an unrelated task for a period of time, rather than taking a break.

To expand upon the concept, introducing a number of distractions into a person's day keeps her from fixating on a specific idea, leading to the introduction of a larger number of ideas, as well as more novel ones. However, there is a cost associated with continual switching, which is the time lost whenever shifting from one activity to another.

Non-Disruptive Innovation

A common assumption is that a high level of innovation is strongly correlated with market disruption. Thus, we assume that a massive change will trigger the decline of established industry players. As an example, the introduction of digital photography led to the rapid decline of Kodak, since its primary source of profits was film. However, this situation only arises when an innovation is targeted at an *existing* market.

The situation is entirely different when an innovation creates a *new* market, where the demand generated is entirely new. In this latter case, management does not have to worry about disrupting its existing operations, with the attendant need to sell off operations or lay off staff. Instead, the creation of a new market means that incremental sales and profits can be layered on top of the company's existing operations, expanding sales and profits. This is a much lower-risk situation, since the firm does not have to worry about cutting into the cash flows from its core operations. Also, since existing operations will not be touched, the decision to pursue an innovation does not directly challenge the existing order, and so meets with little internal resistance. And further, the creation of an entirely new market means that the company is not going head-to-head with any established market leaders – since there aren't any. With no need to battle competitors for supremacy, the odds of success are greatly increased. Finally, by using non-disruptive innovation, the company does not run afoul of any social interest groups that might lobby the government to impose rules in order to preserve jobs; this situation is most likely when disruption will cause the loss of a large number of jobs – witness the backlash from city governments when Uber and Lyft began to hurt local taxi concessions.

The probability of developing a non-disruptive innovation will depend on the type of solution being pursued. For example, if a business is attempting to create a breakthrough solution to an existing problem, it will likely disrupt existing markets, since other organizations are already providing solutions in that area. Thus, the development of GPS mapping systems solved the problem of storing bulky road maps in a car, but also destroyed the map-making business. A similar scenario unfolded when smart phones disrupted the market for flashlights, since this feature is included in smart phones. However, if the goal is to identify an entirely new problem and provide a good solution to it, then no disruption occurs, unless there is an adjacent industry that provides peripheral solutions.

This discussion does not mean that a company should avoid investments in disruptive innovations. After all, these types of innovations can trigger significant increases in market share and spread confusion among the competition. Also, if the company does not pursue disruptive innovations, it is entirely possible that competitors will, resulting in a downturn in the company's affected operations. Consequently, it makes the most sense to pursue both disruptive and non-disruptive innovation opportunities.

Organizational Design Issues

It is not easy to define the softer qualitative aspects of a company's culture that are supportive of innovation. Does the presence of a foosball table or free lunches contribute to or hinder innovation? However, there are some aspects of an organization's *design* that can have more definitive impacts (positive or negative) on innovation, which primarily focus on creating incentives that support innovation. They are:

- *Compensation linkage to projects.* The compensation being paid to those employees involved in innovation projects should be directly linked to the outcome of their projects, rather than the position they hold within the firm. For example, if a team develops a cure for a specific type of dementia, they should be richly compensated for doing so. This compensation may take many forms, including bonuses, pay boosts, and stock options. A variation not involving money is to issue awards for the most innovation solutions.
- *Project fit.* Employees are more productive and innovative when their skills and experience closely dovetail with a project. Conversely, when an employee is not a good fit, he or she tends to spend a lot of time trying to figure out how to *not* be on the project, which is a comprehensive waste of resources. Thus, it can be useful to evaluate who is struggling on a project, to see if they should be assigned to a different task that more closely matches their skills and experience.
- *Impact of lobbying on promotions.* In an environment where office politics is the deciding factor in whether an employee is promoted or given a pay raise, it is quite likely that employees will spend a significant amount of their time engaged in office politics to improve their chances of a favorable outcome. If so, this takes time away from their work on innovation activities. Conversely, when office politics is *not* seen as a deciding factor, the innovation outcome should benefit. One way to minimize office politics is to have an independent party, such as a manager from a different office, make an impartial decision in regard to promotions.

- *Organizational structure.* When a business has many layers in its organizational structure (which is common in a hierarchical organization), there are many promotional opportunities for the multitude of management positions. If so, employees will be more likely to spend a large part of their time angling for these positions. Conversely, when this is *not* the case, where nearly everyone is at the same level within the company, then there are few management positions available, so employees are more likely to focus on their work – such as innovation activities.

> **Note:** When a business has a flat organizational structure, this is great for its innovation efforts – but only if the management team is strong; since there are so few people in management, their competency level needs to be quite high.

- *Salary step-ups.* When there are massive pay increases associated with promotions, employees will be more likely to spend their time lobbying for promotions. Conversely, when the pay range within a business is relatively small, employees will be more likely to work on their innovation activities, especially when doing so could earn them a large bonus. A logical addition to this concept is to minimize any management perks, so that employees will see less value in being a manager.

In summary, a number of organizational design issues can have a direct impact on the propensity of employees to engage more (or less) in innovation-oriented activities.

Organizational Culture Issues

A business that displays certain cultural characteristics is more likely to generate innovations on a consistent basis. Conversely, the absence of these characteristics can act as a roadblock that makes it difficult for all but the most determined advocates to complete innovation projects. The key culture issues to encourage are:

- *Celebrate failure.* Innovation failures are treated as an opportunity to gather useful knowledge, rather than a stain on the careers of everyone involved. Management realizes that most innovations will fail, so employees need to be encouraged to keep trying, as long as doing so results in valuable information.
- *Do not tolerate incompetence.* The flip side of celebrating failure is recognizing when the failure is related to the incompetence of the researcher involved in a project. Incompetence may be related to sloppy thinking, mediocre technical skills, or bad work habits. When this is the case, management will need to upgrade the staff. In other words, a business must both set and clearly articulate high performance standards for its staff; if those standards cannot be met, then terminations should be enacted.

> **Note:** The needs of the innovation staff may change over time, perhaps calling for a different skill set. If so, a company will need to either lay off those project members who are no longer qualified, or shift them into roles for which they are better suited – but they should not be involved in innovation efforts.

- *Establish psychological safety.* Employees should feel that they can speak openly about problems without being targeted with reprisals. When this is the case, people are more likely to speak up about problems found, and to expound alternative viewpoints. This is not always the easiest environment, since it also means that criticism can fly in all directions.
- *Own decisions.* The best innovation teams are not afraid to make decisions, and to own those decisions if the outcomes are poor. This approach is better than consensus, which requires too much time and results in the spreading of responsibility across a group, making it difficult to pin down who has made a decision.
- *Be culturally flat.* In a culturally flat organization, employees have considerable latitude to make decisions. This approach works well, because employees (not their bosses) have access to the most relevant information, and so are in the best position to generate higher-quality ideas.
- *Set innovation goals.* Force the organization to continually push for more innovation by setting revenue goals that are tied to sales from new products.
- *Invest heavily.* A healthy investment in research and development does not guarantee successful products, but it does increase the odds of success.
- *Kill projects.* There are only so many resources available to invest in innovation, so periodically review all outstanding projects to see if any should be killed; doing so frees up cash to invest in more promising opportunities. This process can be hastened by devising "killer experiments" that increase the probability of exposing a concept's flaws. The use of killer experiments allows a business to cycle through more ideas more quickly. Also, when bonuses are paid for good ideas, the use of killer experiments allows employees to identify failed bets and move past them quickly to other ideas that could be more profitable to them.
- *Conduct post mortems.* Team leaders should spend a significant amount of their time dissecting both failed and successful projects. The insights gleaned from this process can then be carried forward into later projects, improving their odds of success.
- *Invest in insights.* Management can hire experts in social media, collaboration, and big data analysis in order to provide insights into possible areas in which further investigation might be warranted.
- *Allow personal projects.* Employees are encouraged to run with their ideas, using company funding. This approach spawns a group of internal entrepreneurs; they use the permissive environment to continually come up with new ideas.

- *Reduce bureaucracy*. Management streamlines the process that employees have to go through to have their ideas approved, and continually reviews it to see if there is a better way. One option is to set up temporary project structures that are allowed to operate under different rules than the rest of the organization. The goal is to keep bureaucracy from becoming an obstacle to innovation.

A concern with the culture issues needed to spur innovation is the relatively common view that a group can be split away from the main business and operate on its own in a "skunk works," where management can more easily control its culture. What they are forgetting is that the people being transferred over are already steeped in the organization's existing culture, and so will be difficult to convert to a new culture. It always requires strong, ongoing management activity to adjust the culture of this group; usually, much more than was originally expected.

Another concern is that the ideal culture is difficult to maintain. For example, a project team might become slack in its efforts and deliver poor results (if any). Or, the use of criticism can devolve into less collegial behavior. Consequently, managers need to be continually cognizant of the current state of affairs, and step in to make adjustments as needed.

Innovation Compensation

We just noted that offering bonuses to those providing valid innovation suggestions is a useful idea. Though it can spur additional innovation activity, additional compensation is usually considered a secondary factor in improving performance. Many employees are more highly motivated by the recognition and status conferred on those who do well, as well as by the intrinsic pleasure associated with having made a difference. In other words, innovation is intrinsically enjoyable, especially when employees can see their ideas being implemented. This viewpoint suggests that a better way to compensate employees is to hold corporate events in which the best ideas and the resulting success stories are celebrated.

Training for Innovation

Some organizations forget that *people* do the innovating, so it makes sense to provide them with ongoing training in how to do so. There are many training topics that can be of assistance, such as:

- How to frame a problem.
- How to brainstorm solutions.
- How to choose ideas.
- How to develop and test a prototype.
- How to convert an idea into a sellable product.

Beyond this basic set of training topics, employees also need detailed information about the markets in which their company sells, such as the types of features that customers value, the price points of competing products, the role of regulation on products, and the threat of competition from adjacent markets. And beyond this knowledge, employees also need to understand how the company's own processes work, ranging from production processes to how goods are delivered from the warehouse to customers.

In short, a broad range of training is needed in order to increase the probability that employees can consistently generate a stream of useful innovations. The ideal knowledge base will allow them to deal with three fundamental issues of product design, which are:

- *Fit to market*. How to design products that closely adhere to customer preferences, while stripping away features that no longer make sense.
- *Fit to manufacturing*. How to design products that are easier and less expensive to build, while still increasing product quality.
- *Fit to industry*. How to extract more value from the supply chain, in the form of lower costs or design suggestions.

Ultimately, the goal of training should be for all employees involved in the innovation process to achieve a high level of technical mastery. This requires not only a significant training budget, but also the incorporation of training achievements into the performance review and compensation process. In addition, senior management needs to fully support this concept, since training (and the time allocated to it) is quite expensive, and requires a long-term commitment.

Setting Aside Time for Innovation

A company may explore the option of letting employees set aside a certain portion of their time to conduct their own innovation projects. For example, Google has (at times) allowed its employees 20% of their time to engage in their own innovation work. The advantage of this approach is that employees may come up with "off the wall" innovations that never would have navigated the normal corporate approval process for project funding. However, setting aside employee time (and possibly other corporate resources) for employee innovation projects can be quite expensive, in terms of the time no longer being directed towards corporate-sponsored activities. Consequently, management should consider the following factors when deciding whether to set aside time for innovation:

- *Who to target*. The ideal employee for designated innovation time is the employee with a high degree of expertise and a penchant for innovation. These people are motivated to experiment, and so are more likely to be quite productive in their innovation activities, with minimal encouragement. The bulk of employees fall somewhere outside of this ideal subset.
- *Additional support*. Management needs to decide upon the extent to which it will provide additional support to employees for their innovation activities, beyond their requirements for ongoing work on behalf of the company. This

might include technology resources, such as computer software, or access to outside experts.

Setting aside time and funding for innovation activities does tend to yield positive results, for several reasons. First, it sends a very strong message that innovation is encouraged, which can be a powerful motivator for those who already have a high degree of expertise and like to innovate. Second, it can be a motivator for somewhat less-skilled personnel to increase their level of expertise. And finally, it increases the level of trust within the organization, since it implies that management trusts employees to make good use of the excess time being blocked out for them.

The concept can be improved upon by setting aside *uninterrupted* time, since higher-quality thinking occurs when a person is totally absorbed with a specific challenge, whether doing so involves observations, meditation, experiments, or conversation. This level of thinking is theoretically possible by setting aside a few minutes for it each day, but it is much more likely when people block out a half-day or full day for it.

There are some cases in which setting aside time for innovation may not be as productive. Critically, those lacking the requisite expertise, and especially those without an interest in innovation, will likely not produce significant results. The level of expertise can be identified in advance, allowing management to exclude these people from the innovation offer. Identifying those without an interest in innovation takes more time, based on the results of the employees who initially take management's offer. The eventual outcome will likely be a relatively small group within the organization that is actively engaged in their own innovation projects.

A cause for concern is when this type of program attracts very few employees, or none at all. In this case, possible questions to investigate are whether the company's hiring practices are adequate for attracting the right types of employees, and whether there is a sufficient level of trust within the organization for employees to believe that the initiative will actually work.

Internal Crowdsourcing

Internal crowdsourcing involves asking a company's employees to contribute ideas to various initiatives. Employees can then work together to devise solutions, and present new ideas to management. This approach is especially useful when specific pockets of expertise are targeted, especially in customer-facing roles where employees are not usually involved in innovation activities.

Internal crowdsourcing can work better than the more common approach of tapping expertise from outside the company, such as consulting firms, because employees are more familiar with the organization and the context within which it operates. Consequently, their suggestions tend to be better tailored to the organization's capabilities, and so are easier to implement. This outcome is especially common when the employees making suggestions are working on the front lines, since they have the best knowledge about the kinds of changes that can realistically be made.

A further benefit of having ongoing internal crowdsourcing events is that the company is sending a message that it values the input of employees, which builds trust within the organization and may reduce employee turnover.

To create a more refined internal crowdsourcing system, consider implementing the following enhancements:

- Ask employees to devise "outside the box" and long-term solutions, rather than incremental adjustments to existing processes, in order to compile a set of higher-quality suggestions.
- For those employees choosing to participate in the challenge, offer some free time in which to develop ideas.
- Allow employees to offer up ideas on an anonymous basis, to avoid any pressure to only make suggestions that benefit their business units. This approach tends to lead to more solutions from lower-level employees.
- State the criteria that will be used to select the best suggestions. For example, if extra points will be assigned to suggestions that can be developed into new products, this knowledge will incentivize employees to come up with more new-product suggestions.
- Offer rewards to groups, rather than individuals, to encourage people to work together to devise solutions. These rewards should be large enough to make employees feel that their suggestions are worth making.
- Offer continual feedback to employees regarding what was done with their suggestions, especially when they are to be implemented. Otherwise, they will think the process was a useless exercise, and so will not be inclined to participate again in the future.

When a large number of ideas are generated from internal crowdsourcing, there needs to be a process in place for sorting through the suggestions, ranking them, and giving feedback. This can be a monumental effort, which ideally should be linked to a searchable database, so that contributors can see the ongoing status of their suggestions.

The Use of Artificial Intelligence in Innovation

There are many possible applications of artificial intelligence (AI) in the workplace, but we are not yet at the point where there is a clear roadmap for how investments in this area will result in instances of innovation. Consequently, there are several ways in which businesses can approach the problem of AI usage. They are:

- *Delay investment*. Management chooses to delay any investment until a later date. This choice may be driven by a high level of uncertainty regarding how AI can be used, or because management has not educated itself regarding the potential of AI. The downside of this approach is in falling well behind competitors who choose to embrace the uncertainty of AI in order to gain a potential edge by exploiting it in an area that might not initially appear to be obvious.

- *Invest in incremental changes.* Management elects to make incremental process improvements in multiple areas within operations, with the intent of driving down costs and increasing productivity by smaller amounts over time. This approach has the benefit of requiring little investment, but carries the risk of falling behind competitors who make significant AI investments in order to gain order-of-magnitude improvements.
- *Invest in the technology.* Management chooses to invest solely in the technology, but does not choose to also restructure jobs to accommodate the resulting changes. This approach assumes that jobs will mostly remain the same, though employees will be more productive. This approach will likely improve customer service or reduce costs, but does not innovatively restructure the workplace to maximize the use of AI.
- *Investment in the technology and personnel.* Management elects to jump into the concept more fully, investing not only in the technology but also in adjusting the structure of jobs to maximize improvements in such areas as product development, customer service, and delivery speed. This approach requires a significant investment in employee training, as well as in hiring new employees with more appropriate skill sets.

While the implication of the preceding options is that one should invest fully in both AI and personnel, that depends on the circumstances. Managers need to understand the risks involved in making too heavy an investment in this area when they don't have a clear understanding of the resulting benefits to be obtained. This risk can be moderated by investigating AI in detail, to gain a clearer understanding of the related risks and benefits. The training of managers could be conducted by subject matter experts who are designated as the initial drivers of AI within the business.

Once there is a reasonably complete understanding of AI and how it applies to the business, management needs to develop a plan that describes the areas to which specific AI applications will be applied, the related investment amounts and implementation timelines, and the expected outcomes. In essence, this plan is a capital budgeting request for the entire AI concept. An addendum may include a discussion of more advanced or theoretical applications to which AI could be applied, which may serve as a roadmap for further investments at a later date.

As is the case with many technology investments, it may be more prudent to initially focus on lower-cost AI applications that are relatively easy to roll out in the short term. Doing so can be used to prove the AI concept, while also building the level of in-house expertise for more advanced projects. A cluster of these easier projects could result in meaningful improvements to the business without incurring an excessive level of risk. This more modest initial approach also tends to have only a modest impact on current jobs, and so calls for a reduced amount of job redesign activity.

Tip: Build as much AI expertise in-house as possible, rather than using consultants, since the most effective use of AI requires a deep knowledge of company processes, which is the purview of employees, not contractors.

The Impact of Cities on Innovation

There tends to be a major concentration of talent in the larger metropolitan areas, such as New York, Boston, Chicago, and San Francisco. This is the case for several reasons. First, an initial cluster of talent tends to attract more talent, so areas such as New York act as magnets for like-minded people. Also, younger people prefer to work in hip downtown locations, rather than in distant suburban office complexes that have relatively fewer amenities. Conversely, suburban and rural areas may also contain talent, but it is much more diffused, making it difficult for businesses to access adequate talent pools, so that their innovation efforts tend to suffer. Logically, it would therefore seem to make sense for a business to set up locations in the major cities, in order to attract the best talent. However, operating a facility in a major city can be quite expensive; this added cost will offset some of the benefits of having access to talent clusters. Consequently, a business may choose from several options, each of which has a different cost structure associated with it. They are:

- *Move the company.* When a business finds that it cannot attract talent throughout its functional areas, it may be time to move to a large city. By doing so, it can greatly increase its talent level throughout the organization. To maximize this effect, it may need to move right into the downtown area, rather than to a suburb. A slight variation is to locate the business relatively close to any college campus in the city from which it expects to hire recruits. However, shifting the entire company can be royally expensive, and may lead to the departure of anyone not willing to move. This cost can be mitigated by splitting the company headquarters, with only innovation-related activities being moved to a designated city location; the rest of the company's functions can remain where they are. An issue to be aware of is that innovations developed at these corporate hubs still need to be pushed out to the rest of the organization, which requires a well-organized implementation capability.

- *Open an innovation lab.* When there are too many risks (and costs) associated with moving an entire company or its headquarters to a city, a reasonable alternative is to open one or more innovation labs in targeted cities. These much smaller facilities are entirely focused on innovation, and so require far fewer employees and a less expensive office footprint. These labs might be focused on process or product improvements, or perhaps concentrate on local business development, or simply as a location from which local research activity is investigated. Given their lower cost, there is much less risk associated with an innovation lab; this being the case, a company may consider opening several of them, to take advantage of the talent clusters in different cities.

- *Organize visits.* The lightest approach is to organize visits by the firm's management team to companies and/or universities in which innovation is occurring. This approach can be useful for jump-starting management thinking about how innovation can help them, perhaps at the level of adjusting their strategic and tactical planning. These visits are more of a foundational, "get the ball rolling" initiative, rather than something that can produce effective innovations on its own. There is a significant risk that the knowledge gained from these visits will be set aside as soon as the management team returns to the home office, so specific implementation responsibilities should be assigned, with follow-up by senior management.

If the innovation lab option is chosen, it can be critical to locate to within a tightly defined area, especially when workers associate a certain district with trendiness. If so, consider renting space on a short-term basis from a coworking company in these select areas – and be willing to move to a coworking location in a trendier area if local tastes change.

Management of Local-Market Innovation Teams

A multi-national company may find that its products, which are frequently designed for large population areas, do not meet the requirements of local markets. For example, a product developed in the United States might sell very well there, and yet perform poorly in India, which has different criteria for product success. When this happens, one alternative is to create local-market innovation teams. Depending on their capabilities, these teams are tasked with either revising existing products or developing entirely new ones that have a better chance of selling in the designated market. This option works best when the following conditions are present:

- The market opportunity should be sufficiently large (or projected to become so) to support the cost of the innovation team. Thus, it may not be economical to create a team in a small country, such as Malta or Liechtenstein, but could be well worth the effort in countries such as India, Indonesia, or Brazil.
- The market should have unique requirements that call for a separate product development effort. For example, a Danish fish processing company that sells pickled herring might have a tough time adapting this product to the Mexican market (or to many other locations, for that matter). Accordingly, it may need to hire a local team to experiment with how herring can be incorporated into the many excellent Mexican fish dinners. The larger the hole in a company's product line that is being addressed, the higher the level of company support will likely be.
- The senior management team needs to provide an exceptionally high level of support to innovation teams at the local level, especially when they have only recently been formed, and so have no reputation within the larger company for developing profitable products. This support includes an adequate amount of funding over a prolonged period of time, so that the team can see its initiatives through to completion (which may require several years).

Management of External Innovators

When a company develops a product that can be used as a platform for additional products (such as the apps sold for Apple iPhones or the games sold on an Xbox), many of those products could be developed by people outside the company. When this is the case, innovation is taking place both outside of the company and outside of its control. How should innovation be managed under these circumstances? There are two alternatives, which are:

- *Collaborative communities*. This approach involves assembling a loosely-organized group that develops product enhancements, typically through joint development efforts. The members of these communities sometimes work for free, being motivated by their need to be part of a larger cause, or to develop a reputation within the field. In this case, the company earns a profit through the increased usage of its platform. This approach is commonly used for open source software solutions, or open source databases, such as Wikipedia.
- *Competitive markets*. This approach involves encouraging multiple parties to develop competing products, from which customers can choose; given the competitive environment, each party is incentivized to develop novel solutions. Each competitor maintains a proprietary interest in its work. These parties are primarily driven by monetary rewards. In this case, the company earns a profit by entering into licensing arrangements with product developers.

In many cases, the only real solution will be the use of competitive markets, since it may not be possible to attract the types of talent needed to develop a collaborative community. If so, the company will need to understand that it is not always dealing directly with end users; instead, outside innovators are using the firm's platform as the basis for sales to customers. In this situation, the company can set standards for the manner in which its platform is to be used, but otherwise stays out of the business of generating sales.

Management of Advanced Research

Many organizations are not interested in early-stage research, because they perceive it as being not only expensive, but also risky – there may be no returns from it at all. It can be quite difficult to extract usable outcomes from this type of activity, unless the process is carefully managed. Here are several ways to improve the odds of success:

- *Focus on specific problem areas*. Rather than funding general research topics, only pursue research in areas where there are solid problems whose solutions could represent major payoffs. Further, the projects selected should always be a good fit with the company's core competencies.
- *Focus on technologies with multiple applications*. Whenever there are multiple possible applications for new ideas, that represents a much better return on research dollars, so these items should be given priority.
- *Attract top talent in tightly-defined areas*. Define the areas in which the company wants to focus its innovation activities, and then bring in the best possible talent that specifically addresses those areas. Another possibility is to limit their time in the group, such as from three to five years; doing so

creates pressure for them to produce. In addition, because people will be leaving after a certain period of time, any mediocre ideas they have been pushing will automatically be terminated when they leave. And finally, it may make sense to offer them a share of the profits if their work leads to viable products.

- *Market the resulting intellectual property.* When research activities uncover new knowledge, always obtain the broadest-possible patents in order to protect this intellectual property; doing so blocks others from claiming rights in the same area. Also, if the company does not plan to use the knowledge in-house, be willing to monetize it with licensing deals.

- *Defend the research unit.* The research unit should not be beholden to any other part of the business, since such a reporting relationship could skew its research priorities. Instead, it should report to a person as high up in the organization as possible. Also, it should be funded consistently from year to year, to reduce employee turnover.

- *Install top management.* The best research leaders are well-respected in their fields and so have an easier time attracting additional top talent to the group. These managers also need to be strong communicators, so that they can secure adequate funding for projects, and can present the value of the research group to the rest of the organization.

- *Release some control.* People work best in an innovative environment when they are allowed some control over their choice of projects and how they want to proceed with research. Giving up this level of control can be difficult, but the best managers understand that this approach makes employees feel more valued, which they tend to reciprocate with additional effort. This does not mean that managers do nothing; they should offer guidance, especially at the start of a project, and are always available for advice. Further, they can set boundaries around a project, such as identifying a market to pursue, or designating another market that is off-limits.

Innovation Development

Once basic research has been completed, the innovation process moves into the development phase. This can be a difficult one for many companies, which flounder through the process of converting ideas into viable products. The following activities can be used to improve the odds of creating products that will be accepted by customers:

1. *Develop multiple prototypes.* Construct a set of simple prototypes (possibly just drawings) that represent several variations on the underlying idea, and test them with customers. Based on their input, construct a minimally-viable prototype and present it to customers again – this will likely shrink the range of viable prototypes. This process is needed to resolve uncertainties about the product offering, which reduces project risk. Also, prototypes are not only cost-effective, but also time-effective, for they require far less time to

construct than a completely operational unit. They can be used to answer a number of questions, such as:

- Would a customer use this product?
- What would be the manner of usage?
- How much would a customer pay for it?
- Will the product work as intended?

2. *Conduct a pilot test.* While still minimizing costs, convert the best of the prototypes into a pilot test, focusing on those key features that are of the most interest to customers.
3. *Bring in customers.* Management can regularly bring customers into its innovation labs, so that they can see the team's prototypes and give immediate feedback on them. Doing so massively increases the number of iterations that development teams can conduct.
4. *Gain customer commitments.* The real proof that an innovation is likely to succeed is when prospective customers are willing to put some skin in the game, such as by putting down a deposit to be one of the first owners. Conversely, if no one is willing to do so, or even be placed on a mailing list to be notified when the product is released, then there may be a customer acceptance problem.
5. *Simplify the concept.* A product that has been refined down to its essentials is much easier to roll out, and within a reasonable time frame. Conversely, as layers of complexity are added to a product, it becomes more difficult to produce.
6. *Construct a business model.* Develop and test each part of a business model, addressing such factors as price points and how to acquire customers.
7. *Prioritize.* There are many competing activities going on in a business at any given time, so management needs to prioritize action around the new product rollout, assigning personnel, money, and other resources to it in sufficient amounts to improve its odds of success.

All of the preceding steps need to be addressed before scaling up the concept into a full-blown product rollout. Even after this has occurred, management still needs to focus on operational efficiencies, since the product will not succeed over the long term unless it can be manufactured at a competitive price that still results in a reasonable margin. A good way to maintain a focus on operational efficiency is to periodically engage in benchmarking activities, to see how other organizations are dealing with the same processes.

Rolling Out Innovations

It can be extremely difficult for a multi-location business to roll out innovations beyond the initial location where they were invented. This is because centers of innovation are built upon a combination of trust between employees and management, where employees know that they can rely on management to provide funding and other resources to investigate new opportunities. In addition, there is usually a history of experimentation, where everyone knows that some failures will be encountered, but that the team will forge onward to find the best solutions, despite any obstacles encountered. Further, everyone involved in an innovation project is working from the same base of process and product knowledge. This scenario breaks down elsewhere, due to differences in products and processes, workplace practices, and how management and employees interact. The following possibilities are suggested for improving the odds of success when rolling out innovations:

- *Define the innovation.* Before conducting any rollout, define the exact nature of the innovation, how it works, and the nature of the expected outcome. This becomes the gold standard that is then rolled out in other locations. This detailed definition is needed to keep variations from being installed in successive locations, resulting in no standardization across the organization. More time spent on this activity tends to reduce the amount of time needed later on, since it reduces the level of uncertainty regarding what is being done.

- *Budget for major travel.* An extensive travel budget will be needed, since it is far easier to settle problems in person than by any technological means, such as email or video conferencing. This is especially important when more complex implementation problems are likely to be encountered, and when local resistance to an installation is expected.

- *Start small.* There can be a significant level of distrust of a new idea that originates elsewhere, so consider starting with quite a small improvement in a few locations, in order to get the local staff used to working with the implementation team. Once the two parties begin to mesh, expand the scope of the projects until the original concepts have been implemented.

- *Establish baseline stability.* The implementation of any innovation brings with it a certain amount of uncertainty regarding job losses, so accompany any innovation announcement with messaging regarding how jobs will not be lost, or at least how employees will be shifted into other work. The messaging should leave minimal doubt about the eventual circumstances in which employees will find themselves. Otherwise, uncertainty and the accompanying resistance to change will likely result in mired projects.

- *Establish high-level support.* A natural side effect of rolling out a project across multiple locations is that it will step on the toes of every manager impacted in the targeted areas, which may result in any number of conflicts. To mitigate these problems, senior-level managers should be assigned to each project, where they have authority over every impacted area, and so can force the settlement of differences in every location. To be effective, these managers will have to maintain a high degree of hands-on involvement with every impacted location.

- *Install high-grade project teams.* When rolling out an installation in multiple locations, a project team is likely to encounter every possible challenge to a successful implementation. To counter these issues, it is essential to have the strongest-possible project teams, led by fully-qualified team leaders who have experience with large-scale rollouts. A good way to develop such expertise is to have a corporate project management department that trains team members and develops common practices for them to follow.

- *Schedule based on applicable expertise.* Installations should not be scheduled for those periods in which enough warm bodies are available to complete the work. Instead, schedule installations around the availability of those people with the most applicable expertise. In essence, the presence of an on-site expert makes it much easier to successfully complete an innovation rollout, while that person's absence is nearly guaranteed to ensure project failure.
- *Minimize the use of outsiders.* Scheduling the time of contractors onto teams introduces one more element of complexity to a project that is likely to already be quite difficult to schedule, so minimize their use to only the most essential personnel, even if doing so will increase the cost of the project somewhat. When it is necessary to bring in contractors, it can make sense to use ones located near the implementation sites, since they will be more culturally aligned with the local employees (especially important when roll outs span several countries).

The probability of success is greater if all of the preceding recommendations are installed, since each one impacts a different problem area commonly encountered with innovation roll outs.

Excessive Innovation Effects

It might seem logical to invest in an ever-increasing array of innovations, effectively blanketing the market with lots of new stuff. By doing so, a company can overwhelm its competition, enter lots of juicy new markets, and position itself as an innovation juggernaut in order to attract the best talent. While this approach might initially seem like a can't-lose option that will yield massive revenues, there are a few cautionary points to consider before embarking upon it. They are:

- *Business complexity.* Greatly expanding the range of products being offered means that the complexity of the business has also increased, since there are now more stock-keeping units and product lines to manage, along with the attendant marketing and distribution requirements. In fact, nearly every part of a business is adversely affected when the number of products issued is expanded.
- *Customer service.* With more products comes an inevitable decline in customer service. This is because more service parts need to be stocked, employees need to be trained in how to repair more products, and customers are more likely to require several interactions with the company in order to have their issues fixed. In short, increased complexity worsens the customer experience.

These issues can increase administrative costs substantially, while also driving away customers. To keep this from happening, while still engaging in enough innovation to enhance the business, follow these rules:

- *Establish a vision*. The company should have a clear vision for what types of innovations it wants to pursue. Any suggestions falling outside of this vision are abandoned at once, since they will not support the direction of the company. Thus, an effective vision statement is one that can be used to decide whether an innovation is valuable, or should be discarded.

- *Rationalize the product line*. Always be aware of the differentiating factors between each product in a product line, so that customers have a clear progression of choices as they go from the bottom to the top of the product offerings. If any proposed addition does not logically fit into the current product line, then do not add it.

- *Integrate innovations*. When innovations are tightly integrated into a company's current product offerings, the customer experience tends to improve. Accordingly, discuss integration opportunities as part of the evaluation of any prospective innovation ideas. For example, a company could evaluate a customer's needs and propose a complete bundle of products that exactly meets his or her requirements. This approach can mean that a proposed new product that cannot easily be integrated into a company's existing offerings is turned down, even though it might generate revenues.

- *Clean up the internal coordination*. If a new product has unusual administrative, production, or distribution requirements, delay its introduction until the related issues have been streamlined to the greatest extent possible. This approach usually allows for a higher degree of automation when dealing with customers, too.

- *Talk to customers*. Converse with customers regularly to ascertain their pain points when dealing with the company. If any of these issues are caused by excessive innovation, deal with the underlying issues at once.

- *Make innovators talk to operations personnel*. The people involved in innovation need to talk to operations personnel to gain a full understanding of the grief they are causing elsewhere in the organization. With this feedback loop in place, products can be adjusted to fit more seamlessly into company operations. A variation on the concept is to establish cross-functional teams that are embedded in the innovation process, which has the same result.

Innovation Metrics

In this section, we focus on a number of metrics relating to innovation, including the economical usage of design platforms and existing components, as well as the time required to develop products, the percentage of new-product sales, and the return on research and development expenditures. However, before settling upon one or more of these metrics as your ideal innovation measurement, consider the needs of the organization and then pick the measurement that best addresses those needs. This selection process should take some time, since there is a risk of publishing metrics that incentivize employees to do the wrong things. When picking measurements, consider the following issues:

- *Measurement duration*. Measure for the long term, rather than the short term. Some innovation effects will not become significant for a long period of time, so it is essential to not rely exclusively on short-term monthly or quarterly measurements.
- *Level of detail*. Innovation cannot be managed at the level of detail used for other processes, so do not measure it too tightly. For example, a measurement targets the incremental improvement in the return on innovation investments, and is used to cut off investments below a specific threshold level (as is the case with many capital budgeting systems). However, innovations may have a layering effect, where one innovation builds upon the positive effects of a prior improvement. If so, using a hard cutoff for investment approvals may not be a good idea.
- *Motivational impact*. Before rolling out a measurement, consider that what gets measured directly impacts what gets done, and what gets done directly impacts who gets rewarded. Thus, altering measurement systems has a direct compensation impact on employees, which will alter their behavior.
- *Linkage to strategy*. Any measurements selected should directly support efforts to achieve the company strategy as it relates to innovation. For example, a strategy of being first to market with a new automated teller machine should be supported by measures that focus on the time required to complete the project, without being sidetracked excessively by other issues.

In the following sub-sections, we describe a number of measurements that can be applied to innovation-related activities.

Allocation of Investments

The decision to invest in an innovation project is a major one, since there may be limited funding available, and not all proposals can be funded. When this is the case, it can be useful to categorize the proposals into such classifications as product line extensions and breakthrough projects. By doing so, management can look at the overall allocations of funding into the various categories and decide whether they meet the risk profile of the business. For example, a 90% allocation to product line extensions is quite conservative, with only 10% of the funding allocated toward "swing for the fences" breakthrough projects. It can be useful to track these allocation percentages over a period of time, to gain a better understanding of management's acceptance of risk.

EXAMPLE

A new CEO has been hired into Aerial Taxi Corporation. He notices that the firm has not generated much of a return on its investments in innovation over the past few years, so he has an analyst create an overview of the firm's investments over the past five years, with investments aggregated into the breakthrough product and product enhancement categories. The results appear in the following table.

	20X5	20X4	20X3	20X2	20X1
Breakthrough products proportion	62%	60%	55%	51%	40%
Product enhancement proportion	38%	40%	45%	49%	60%

He then compares this information to the following analysis, which shows the return on investment for the two classifications:

	20X5	20X4	20X3	20X2	20X1
Breakthrough products ROI	3%	-17%	2%	5%	-12%
Product enhancement ROI	16%	11%	23%	15%	18%

From these analyses, it is apparent that his predecessor was desperate to achieve a breakthrough product success, and so kept pouring more money into an innovation category that had historically yielded very low returns. He takes immediate steps to drastically alter the investment strategy in favor of more product enhancements.

A variation on this concept is to track the allocation of investments into projects that are targeted at products to be offered in entirely new markets.

Roadblock Analysis

A company may experience issues with innovation projects constantly being halted for various reasons. If so, a reasonable measurement would be the percentage of time a project is waiting for inputs or resources, as opposed to currently being in process. This information can then be used to drill down into the underlying issues, so that management can take steps to clear up the various roadblocks.

EXAMPLE

Finchley Fireworks is working on a new product that produces a holographic image of fireworks displays, rather than relying on the real thing. An analysis of the product reveals that, during its first six months, it was waiting for inputs or resources 82% of the time. An analyst breaks down these roadblocks in the following table:

Roadblock Item	% of Time
Waiting for technological review by IT department	30%
Waiting for delivery of beta test version from supplier	28%
Waiting for executive approval	16%
Waiting for capital budgeting analysis	8%
Total	82%

The CEO takes personal responsibility for the executive approval delay, and works with the IT and accounting departments to accelerate the speed of their activities relating to the project.

Design Cycle Time

In some industries, a distinct competitive advantage can be gained by designing new products within the shortest possible period of time. By doing so, a business can launch products ahead of competitors and gain market share.

To calculate design cycle time, subtract the design start date from the product launch date for each product. Note that this time period encompasses not only the work of the product design staff, but also the time required to procure components, manufacture goods, distribute goods in preparation for sale, and launch a marketing campaign. Thus, the responsibility for design cycle time rests with many departments, not just the product design team. The calculation is:

Product launch date – Design start date

If the design cycle time is aggregated across all products, a number of minor product updates could artificially give the appearance of an extremely rapid cycle time. To avoid this skewed result, differentiate between minor updates and major new products, and measure their cycle times separately.

A possible issue with an excessive focus on design cycle time is that products may be released to the market before they have been fully tested, possibly resulting in excessive warranty claims or even product recalls. Thus, it can be useful to review the trend line for warranty costs in conjunction with design cycle time.

EXAMPLE

The president of Grubstake Brothers is concerned that the Japanese competition is developing new backhoes at a much faster pace than Grubstake, resulting in lost sales. He initiates sweeping product development changes, with the following results in design cycle time:

Year	Average Design Cycle Time
20X1	304 days
20X2	291 days
20X3	268 days

Thus, over the three-year measurement period, the company has succeeded in shrinking the average cycle time by 12%.

Number of Design Platforms

The most efficient way to develop a range of products is to use a common design platform as the basis for as many products as possible. Each design platform has a common set of parts, can be produced by a production line that is specifically constructed for it, and is supported by a group of experienced design engineers. This leads to the following advantages for each product developed using an existing platform:

- A smaller incremental investment in inventory, since many of the component parts are already in stock.
- Less time to ramp up production, since the manufacturing capability already exists.
- Less risk of warranty claims, since the underlying platform has already been tested by users.
- Less time to design new products, since designs may only be slight tweaks of existing products.

Clearly, measuring the number of design platforms can be a key consideration for a company that wants to rationalize a wildly proliferated set of products. A variation on the measurement is to track the number of products using each design platform.

EXAMPLE

A new CEO has just been hired to run Grizzly Golf Carts, which is known for its robust designs catering to overweight golfers. The CEO comes from a lean manufacturing background where vehicle designs are based on the minimum number of design platforms. He finds that Grizzly offers 30 models based on 15 different design platforms. He immediately slashes 10 of the products, because they not only have poor sales, but also operate on unique platforms. Of the remaining 20 models, he orders the staggered redesign of 14 models, so that they are based on one of the five remaining platforms. At the end of this process, the CEO expects to have 20 models that are based on five platforms, for an average of four models per platform.

Reused Components Percentage

A company can reduce the complexity of its operations by using the same components in multiple products. Doing so yields the following benefits:

- Fewer items to maintain in the inventory records
- Can purchase a smaller number of items in bulk, resulting in volume purchase discounts
- Fewer suppliers to deal with
- Less likely to have obsolete inventory items, since parts can be repurposed if a product is eliminated
- More historically-based knowledge of component failure rates

In short, there are many reasons to push the design staff in the direction of creating new products that reuse existing components.

To calculate the reused components percentage, aggregate the number of existing parts in the bill of materials of a new product and divide by the total number of parts in the bill. Ideally, the existing parts listed in the numerator are only those that have been specifically approved in advance for re-use in new products. The formula is:

$$\frac{\text{Number of existing parts in bill of materials of new product}}{\text{Total number of parts in the bill of materials}}$$

This measurement only works if the engineering department has issued a comprehensive bill of materials.

If too much emphasis is based on this measurement, there may be a tendency for the design staff to not experiment with new materials or suppliers. To mitigate this concern, consider assigning some of the staff to an ongoing review of replacement components that can be adopted throughout the company's various product lines.

EXAMPLE

The Black Cat Ladder Company has a strong incentive to reuse existing parts for new ladder designs, since some components have been certified to not collapse – a key element of a ladder. Consequently, when the design manager envisioned a No Slip ladder, the reused components percentage was mandated to be at least 85%, with new components only being allowed for the grid pads used on the ladder steps to reduce slippage. As a result, 34 parts out of 38 were reused, which is an 89% reused components percentage.

Percentage of New-Product Sales

One way to force employees to continually develop new products is to set a target for what proportion of sales will come from new products, typically on a rolling basis that looks back anywhere from one to three years. Doing so forces them to look for larger product opportunities that can have a notable impact on sales.

To measure the percentage of new-product sales, divide all sales related to new stock-keeping units by total net sales for the measurement period. We use the creation of a new stock-keeping unit as the most likely threshold for a product being considered sufficiently new that it is given a separate identification. The formula is:

$$\frac{\text{Sales from new stock-keeping units}}{\text{Total net sales}}$$

This measurement is most commonly used in markets where there is such intense competition that the only way to maintain sales is to continually release a stream of new products. If the marketplace is instead a staid one, it may not be necessary to place such a focus on new product sales.

EXAMPLE

Dude Skis manufactures wide skis most applicable to powder skiing. The buyers of these skis are a fickle lot, basing their decisions mostly on the graphics laminated to the tops of the skis. Consequently, Dude must continually issue new models with different graphics in order to appeal to its buyers. The company targets having 75% of its sales come from new models each year. In the most recent year, $3,400,000 of its total sales of $4,850,000 were from the sale of new ski designs. This represents a proportion of 70% of new models, which is below the corporate target. Accordingly, the company hires an additional graphics designer to develop more ski graphics.

Innovation Pipeline Strength

It can be useful to evaluate the strength of the new product pipeline, especially in industries where product cycles are short. When these cycles are short, management needs to pay much more attention to whether there are sufficient new product ideas coming through the development pipeline to maintain or expand sales. This pipeline can be measured by evaluating the revenue-generating potential of products still in the pipeline. The aggregate amount of the median estimated revenue for each product is the innovation pipeline strength.

There are several concerns with this measurement. First, it can be quite difficult to arrive at any revenue-generating potential measurements that turn out to be reasonably accurate, though estimates can be made based on the revenue outcomes of similar products that are already being sold. Also, the prospects for commercial failure must also be evaluated, so that outright failures are identified. A final concern is that revenue-generating potential does not necessarily equate to profit potential, since the margins associated with new products may differ from what the company is currently experiencing with its other products. Despite these issues, it can still be useful to derive innovation pipeline strength estimates at regular intervals, to see if the business has sustainable revenues over the medium-term.

> **Tip:** It can make sense to report the low, median, and high revenue estimates for the innovation pipeline, so that management can better understand the risk of sales differing substantially from the median estimate.

Patent Utilization Rate

Evidence of an effective innovation effort is a high proportion of patents that are being utilized. This is calculated as the number of patents that a firm uses, divided by the total number of unexpired patents that it owns. In many companies, it is not common for even half of all patents to be used.

A low patent utilization rate does not necessarily mean that a company's innovation processes have performed poorly, only that it has not chosen to bring products to market that can utilize the patents. A good alternative in this situation is to conduct a search to see if the unused patents can be sold or licensed to other parties. Thus, the patent utilization rate can be used as an indicator that a business should interact with other parties on a more regular basis to see if someone else can use its patents.

EXAMPLE

Creekside Industrial has developed a number of patents related to its lithium-ion batteries. However, the firm is about to downgrade its emphasis on this field, in favor of higher-capacity molecular batteries. Consequently, the CEO is not surprised when an analysis of the firm's patent portfolio reveals that only 12% of its patents are being used. Accordingly, she contacts a patent broker to see if any licensing deals can be arranged with other parties in the battery industry who might be interested in buying the patents or entering into licensing deals.

Return on Research and Development

One of the most puzzling aspects of funding allocation is how much money to invest in research and development. Typically, the same amount spent historically is spent again in the current period, or else funding is based on a percentage of sales, or perhaps on the amounts being spent by competitors. An alternative approach is to calculate the return on funds spent on research and development. This approach is concerned with the effectiveness of funds spent, rather than with the gross amount of cash plowed into research and development. To calculate the return on research and development, follow these steps:

1. Aggregate the net profit from licensing deals generated by research and development.
2. Aggregate the net profit from the sale of all products generated by research and development.

41

3. Aggregate the net profit from all lawsuits related to intellectual property derived from research and development.
4. Add together the preceding items and divide by the research and development expense (which should include the cost of filing for and maintaining patents).

The formula is:

$$\frac{\text{Licensing net profit + New product net profit + Lawsuit net profit}}{\text{All research and development expenses}}$$

The expenditures for research and development that led to the various forms of income noted in the numerator of this calculation may have occurred several years in the past. Consequently, this measurement should span a long period of time. For example, consider a trend line analysis, on which each data point represents one year of activity.

EXAMPLE

High Noon Armaments has spent $5,000,000 per year on research and development for the past five years, and the president is interested in the type of return the company has achieved from this investment. In the most recent year, the company has earned $750,000 from licensing the use of a new form of flashless gunpowder, as well as $250,000 from a lawsuit settlement, and $1,500,000 from the ongoing sale of a newly-developed sniper rifle to the military. Thus, the return on research and development for the current year is:

$$\frac{\$750,000 \text{ Profit} + \$1,500,000 \text{ New product profit} + \$250,000 \text{ Lawsuit profit}}{\$5,000,000 \text{ Research and development investment}}$$

$$= 50\% \text{ Return on research and development}$$

Innovation Personnel Turnover Rate

A business should be making significant and sustained investments in its innovation personnel, since these people are the primary drivers of its growth and competitiveness. Ideally, this group should have an extremely low turnover rate, so that the business is not losing its investment in them. Measuring turnover for these people should take into account the following factors:

- *Incompetence*. Some innovation personnel are simply not able to innovate, and so should be let go as expeditiously as possible, so that they can be replaced by new hires with more potential. This means that there can certainly be a minimum level of expected turnover.
- *Reasons*. Some reasons for turnover are benign, such as a spouse taking a job on the other side of the planet, while others could be an indicator of a problem, such as being hired away by a competitor for a higher salary. Consequently, any measurement should include a summary of the exit interview conducted with each person who has left.

EXAMPLE

Glow Atomic operates the world's most advanced experimental fusion reactor, using a new spherical tokamak design. Its design staff is comprised of 40 physics PhDs from the world's best universities. Given the extremely advanced nature of its work, Glow's CEO is concerned whenever one of the design team leaves the company. Accordingly, he receives a rolling 12-month report of all departures from the firm, which includes commentary on the underlying reasons. The latest report is as follows:

Name	Departure Date	Commentary
Becquerel, Pierre	February 15, 20X1	Received inheritance and retired
Cherenkov, Abraham	June 21, 20X1	Hired by General Fusion for twice the salary
Schwinger, Albert	October 2, 20X2	Fired for being unable to work with colleagues

Summary

An effective innovation program can have a spectacular effect on the financial results of a business, but it can be quite difficult to achieve, and even more difficult to maintain over the long term. To achieve good results, management first needs to focus attention on those areas of the business that are most likely to profit from innovation, which means that it weeds out improvement suggestions that do not support the strategic direction of the business. Then it needs to decide whether it will only work internally on innovation activities, or whether the organization should be open to input from the outside, which may include paying for improvements that originate elsewhere, or entering into research partnerships with other companies. Then, to have a functioning innovation effort, it needs to design the organization and create a corporate culture that is conducive to a thriving innovation environment – which can be difficult not only to create, but also to maintain over the long term. Next, it needs to decide how much funding to make available for innovation activities, which should include a discussion of the apportionment of investments among more-risky and less-risky projects. And finally, management needs to create a well-designed system for fully implementing any new innovations, including their roll-out across the organization within a reasonable period of time. A measurement system will be needed, so that management can keep tabs on the progress of the various projects, how well patents are being exploited, how innovations are contributing to revenues, and so forth. If these activities can be organized properly, then a business has gone a long ways towards making itself a competitive force in its chosen markets.

Glossary

B

Benchmarking. A process for comparing the policies, procedures, products, and processes of a business to those of other firms or to standard measurements.

Bill of materials. A record of the raw materials, sub-assemblies and supplies used to construct a product.

I

Incremental innovation. When management elects to make small, iterative improvements.

Innovation. A new idea or creative thinking, which is then practically applied.

Internal crowdsourcing. The process of asking employees to contribute ideas to various initiatives.

S

Strategic investment. A risky new venture being run within an established business.

Index

www.ingramcontent.com/pod-product-compliance
Lightning Source LLC
Chambersburg PA
CBHW080722220326
41520CB00056B/7364